Outpouring

Experiencing The Fresh Power Of The Holy Spirit In Your Life!

"I Will Pour Out My Spirit..."
Acts 2:17

SONJIA B. DICKERSON

Outpouring

Sonjia B. Dickerson

ISBN: 978-1-7330235-0-4
Copyright © 2019
Printed in the United States

All Scripture quotations are taken from the New King James Version of the Bible. Copyright © 1982 by Thomas Nelson, Inc. Used by permission.

Dedication

This book is dedicated to my Lord and Savior Jesus Christ, Whose Presence I live for. So grateful to be His servant. I will spend my life worshipping at my Lord's feet.

To my husband Kevin, my best friend and greatest supporter. Thank you for being amazing!
I love you to life!

To our son Kevin, and daughters Cherese and Faith, thanks for all the joy you bring to my life and your constant love and support.

To my siblings and their spouses George and Mary Reaves, Ronald and Fanchion Blumenberg, Leon and Alice Blumenberg, you've always set the example and pushed me to be my best! Thanks so much!

In loving memory of my Dear Parents
Elder William and Mother Mary Blumenberg
Who sacrificed so much for me to be successful.

In loving memory of my
Dear Father In Law & Mother In Law
Elder Chester and Mother Beatrice Dickerson
Who accepted me, loved me, and encouraged me.

To Mother Almyra Battles
Who continues to provide support and guidance.

To my Literary Team, Lula Lott who labors tirelessly for the Kingdom and Mary Frazier for your willingness to serve. Thanks for your dedication to this work and ministry.

To every person who is hungry for more of the Holy Spirit, desperate for God's Power, and would love to experience God's Presence...
this book is for you!!!

Introduction

It felt like an earthquake. There was a rumbling, a shaking. The sounds filled the air. The closer you got, the louder it got. From afar the rumblings were just tremors, but when the door opened, and you walked in, there was a full-blown seismic event taking place. The room. The room. Small, cramped, planks of wood posing as benches. It could barely hold 80 people but more than 300 were crammed into every nook, every corner, every inch of space.

The building was inconspicuous. The neighborhood that surrounded it, was crime-ridden and poor. From the outside the building didn't look like much. Peeling paint, a decaying edifice; but that didn't matter. All that mattered was what was going on inside. All that mattered was what all those people were waiting for. Why would over 300 people cram themselves in a room for seven days? What were they looking for? What were they waiting on?

They had been at 312 Azusa St. for seven days now. All day. Praying, praising, singing, worshipping, and preaching. They were in a room, waiting on it. The sound. It was deafening. Full of fervor and passion. Every stomp of their feet on that wooden floor more powerful than any bass drum.

The clapping of their hands in unison. It felt like thunder. Seven days of non-stop thunder. And then…it happened. Lightening.

May 1906…. the thunder met the lightening. What happened? William Seymour knew. The preacher, the founder of this Azusa St. Revival knew what was taking place. He had experienced it before. Earlier that year, Seymour attended a Bible school ran by his mentor Charles Parham. It was there in Houston where Seymour would experience it. He learned about it and then took what he had learned and made his way to Los Angeles. What started out at the home of two of his followers expanded to that little building on Azusa Street. For seven days, the people prayed and sang and worshipped, and praised God. For seven days, there were signs, wonders, healings, and miracles. Seven days…and it happened.

What happened?

The Outpouring.

The Bible school in Houston, the Revival on Azusa St, wasn't the first experience of the Outpouring. The first and greatest Outpouring started in the Upper Room on the Day of Pentecost.

The saints were gathered there on one accord and in one place, and it was there that the first Outpouring of the Holy Spirit occurred.

Acts 2:1-4 (KJV)
[1] And when the day of Pentecost was fully come, they were all with one accord in one place.
[2] And suddenly there came a sound from heaven as of a rushing mighty wind, and it filled all the house where they were sitting.
[3] And there appeared unto them cloven tongues like as of fire, and it sat upon each of them.
[4] And they were all filled with the Holy Ghost, and began to speak with other tongues, as the Spirit gave them utterance.

There have been other events since then where people have gathered in various cities and experienced a special Outpouring of the Holy Spirit. Often those around didn't understand what was happening. The media tried to cover it but was hard pressed to explain the emotions exhibited by
those attending these events. The reaction on the Day of Pentecost was similar.

The bystanders assumed those experiencing the Outpouring of the Holy Spirit were drunk!

Often when behaviors can't be explained they are instead placed in negative categories.

However that day shook the entire world and was the fulfillment of the promise Jesus gave before he ascended to the Father.

John 14:26 (KJV)
[26]But the Comforter, which is the Holy Ghost, whom the Father will send in my name, he shall teach you all things, and bring all things to your remembrance, whatsoever I have said unto you.

John 15:26
[26]But when the Comforter is come, whom I will send unto you from the Father, even the Spirit of truth, which proceedeth from the Father, he shall testify of me:

The Day of Pentecost was the fulfillment of the promise made by Jesus to His followers!

That was then, but what about now? Where is the Outpouring and how do I become a part of it? Is it at a certain geographical location? Where is the Azusa of our day? Is there a restriction on who can participate? In the following pages you will find all these answers and more, as we experience a defining moment in all our lives. The Outpouring!!!

Table Of Contents

Chapter One

What Is Outpouring?

Outpouring

Experiencing The Fresh Power Of The Holy Spirit In Your Life!

"I Will Pour Out My Spirit..."
Acts 2:17

The word carries with it the connotation of abundance. Excess. Overflow. Plenty. More than enough. The word outpour tells us that whatever is being dispensed, it's more than enough to exceed our capacity. For example, "The outpouring of love in my time of difficulty was so great I could hardly believe it." My favorite definition is "it's a spontaneous flood of affection and support."

While in most instances a "flood" is an indicator of something negative, here it is a positive. This "flood", this Outpouring not only fills us to capacity; but it causes us to overflow. The overflow, we can try to take it all, but as it overwhelms us it leaves us with only one option: surrender. Bask in it, as it cascades all around us, in us, and through us. In that moment it feels as if time stands still and our problems, fears, and disappointments seem small compared to the overwhelming, refreshing power of God.

The journey to the place of the Outpouring is an individual one. Taking the journey is your responsibility.

This journey is not one that is built on happenstance or coincidence; it's a journey built on intent.

Everything about the journey has to be intentional.

It's important to be intentional about the environment we are in. We must evaluate if that environment will yield a positive or negative outpouring.

Will it leave us full, or empty? Fixed or broken? Healed or further injured? It's also important that we be intentional about the people we allow to share in the journey. There will be those around us who will not understand what the Outpouring is or why it's so important to you to receive it. They will attempt to discourage you by telling you "it doesn't take all of that". So be intentional about who you allow in your space.

After experiencing the Outpouring from God we are always better. The refreshing which only the

Holy Spirit gives includes the tremendous power to impact every area of our lives.

It's amazing how the Holy Spirit weaves Himself throughout all of our problems, challenges, and situations giving us guidance and comfort.

It's also amazing how the Holy Spirit brings joy, peace, excitement, reassurance, and blessing. So, we pursue, with everything in us this moment, this shower, this flood, this time of *OUTPOURING.*

My Next Steps

1. _____

_____

_____

2. _____

_____

_____

3. _____

_____

_____

_____

Notes

Chapter Two

You Must Show Up!

Outpouring

Experiencing The Fresh Power Of The Holy Spirit In Your Life!

"I Will Pour Out My Spirit..."
Acts 2:17

To receive the Outpouring, you must participate. There is a personal responsibility involved. Often, we expect things to just be dropped down in our vicinity and we benefit from it. Even though we haven't put in the work necessary to receive what we're looking for we think we're entitled to it. There will be NO withdrawing from a bank, when you have not made any deposits. There will be no weight loss benefits from a gym membership unless you go there to work out. There will be no graduation, without study. And the list goes on of things you simply will not attain without putting the work in. I'm concerned that our culture often advances the notion that somehow, we "deserve something" even if we haven't made the effort necessary to attain it. If you want to receive the *Outpouring* your participation is needed.

James 2:26
[26]For as the body without the spirit is dead, so faith without works is dead also.

Many times, we are believing for things and asking

God for things but making no effort to achieve the goal. You must take the first step!

Of course, God will be there to hold you up, encourage your heart, give you direction but you must "get moving"
first. No war has ever been won while the soldiers sat idly by.

The wars were won while they were fighting. You will need to fight for this outpour. Fight what? The distractions all around us. The things that pull us away from God. The busyness of the day. The words people have spoken to discourage you. You will need to fight complacency and tradition. Outpourings are unscripted and dynamic. Are you willing to get out of your comfort zone and do what it takes to experience the OUTPOUR?

My Next Steps

1. _____

_____

_____

2. _____

_____

_____

3. _____

_____

_____

Notes

Joshua 1:9

"Have not I commanded thee? Be strong and of a good courage; be not afraid, neither be thou dismayed:for the LORD thy God is with thee whithersoever thou goest".

Chapter Three

The Foundation That
Never Needs Repair

Outpouring

Experiencing The Fresh Power
Of The Holy Spirit In Your Life!

"I Will Pour Out My Spirit..."
Acts 2:17

Every time there is some major storm home repair businesses will come and try to solicit your business. They know that because of the storm there will be damage to the homes and businesses in the area. Often the homes are uninhabitable, and the businesses can no longer operate until the repairs are made. There are major storms in our lives as well. Sickness, death, job loss, divorce, pressure, emotional distress are all challenges which can cause an upheaval of catastrophic proportions. However, there is one foundation that never cracks. It doesn't need repair in the sense that others must get involved. Only you and God are needed and that is the foundation of prayer.

Prayer is the first step to experiencing the outpour. Prayer is one of the most precious gifts the Christian receives. The ability to communicate with God is nothing short of amazing. What an honor to share our innermost thoughts, desires, and even insecurities in such an intimate way with the Creator of the universe. This priceless gift is often underutilized and even forgotten has given us.

Prayer is direct communication with God. It's not only thinking about Him, but also addressing God.

The very thought is humbling. Who are we to address God? But this is the privilege He has given us.

Our minds, our bodies, our emotions, and our very souls get involved in this discourse. When done correctly, prayer is a time of total transparency and vulnerability.

Prayer is a place of safety, pain, joy, resolution, and challenge. Often all at the same time.

We bring our issues to God who is able to solve them. We bring our questions to God who has the answers. We bring our lives to Him who gives us life. Prayer is a conversation. Talk a while. Listen a while.

More listening than talking. Never forgetting to listen because every answer we need is found in this most valuable conversation with God Almighty.

Even Jesus prayed and taught His disciples to do the same.

His example of prayer is encouraging and powerful. One might think there surely would be no need for the Savior of the world to pray.

However, Jesus made prayer a vital part of His life. When Jesus prayed, He did so with great passion and power.

When Jesus prayed He always did so with utmost sincerity and humility. There was never a time when Jesus prayed out of tradition or to impress those around Him. Instead His prayers were sincere, and God focused. As opposed to being self-centered, He was God centered.

The victory that He gained as a result of praying is a compelling argument for incorporating prayer into our daily lives. Often, we look around us with dismay as we see the unfortunate things happening in our world.

As we see those who are less fortunate, those who are suffering, those who have gone astray, or those addicted to drugs or alcohol we wonder what the answer is. The answer will come through prayer.

II Chronicles 7:14
[14]If my people, which are called by my name, shall humble themselves, and pray, and seek my face, and turn from their wicked ways; then will I hear from heaven, and will forgive their sin, and will heal their land.

Spending time with God in prayer opens the door for the outpouring. Hearing God's voice allows you to be sensitive to the move of the Holy Spirit.

That simply means you anticipate and expect to feel the power of God. Pray often. Pray sincerely. Pray about everything. Ask for direction and guidance. Every answer you need you will discover through prayer.

My Next Steps

1. _____

_____

_____

2. _____

_____

_____

3. _____

_____

_____

Notes

<u>Acts 4:31</u>

"And when they had prayed,
the place was shaken where
they were assembled together;
and they were all filled with
the Holy Ghost, and they
spake the word of God with
boldness".

Chapter Four

Walk By Faith

Outpouring

Experiencing The Fresh Power Of The Holy Spirit In Your Life!

"I Will Pour Out My Spirit..."
Acts 2:17

With our foundation of prayer secure, the next step to experiencing the Outpouring is to Walk by Faith. The Bible emphasizes that faith is an important component in the life of the believer.

Hebrews 11:6 (KJV)
[6]But without faith it is impossible to please Him: for he that cometh to God must believe that he is, and that He is a rewarder of them that diligently seek Him.

Faith is a spiritual law and principle established by God. Faith is critical to the success of our spiritual lives. Faith is a strong confidence and anticipation that God is going to do everything He promised in His Word. You must be persistent in prayer and stay with your faith until they produce results. Faith will produce results over time.

You can't expect it to work overnight. In order to achieve any goal or dream; it's going to take time. If you focus only on your circumstances, and you rely upon your own ingenuity to get out; then your defeat is assured. Our victory lies in focusing our faith in Jesus! That's why the Bible tells us in Hebrews 12:2, "Looking (focusing) unto Jesus who is the author and the finisher of our faith".

When we focus on Jesus then our circumstances lose their power to control our existence or the quality of our lives.

We must realize that the circumstances are not our source. God is our source. Circumstances are what we go through; but it is God who brings us through. If we could get ourselves out or make things happen in our own way; then there would be no need for faith.

Faith is activated by our words! You must speak by faith the outcome you desire. And when you say it, BELIEVE IT! If it is a righteous desire that lines up with the Word of God, then our Lord promised, He would bring it to pass.

2 Cor. 5:7 (KJV)
[7] (For we walk by faith, not by sight)

The Apostle Paul told us on three separate occasions in the New Testament that the "righteous shall live by faith." Shall live. That word shall means that it isn't a suggestion or an option for the believer.

We are commanded to live by faith. What does it mean to live by faith? Living by faith means basing my entire existence upon the Word of God.

It is expecting my life and the things in my life to line up with who the Word says I am and what the Word says I should receive. How do we live by faith? First, we must study the Word of God.

The Bible is our textbook. Don't be afraid to write in it. Make notes in the margins. Highlight passages.

Treat it like an English or geometry text and study it so you can be properly prepared for the tests of life.

2 Tim. 2:15 (KJV)
[15]Study to shew thyself approved unto God, a work-
man that needeth not to be ashamed, rightly dividing
the word of truth.

Make a commitment to daily Bible reading and listening to the Word of God. There are several apps that are a great help in the area of Bible Study. Our faith is built when we study God's Word. How do we live by faith? Secondly, we must believe the Word of God.

It's one thing to study the Word; but then the question becomes do you believe what you read? Do you believe that He will never leave you nor forsake you?

Do you believe that you are the head and not the tail? Do you believe that whatever we ask in His Name, it shall be done? Living by faith means believing that every promise found in the Word is available to you even today. How do we live by faith? Lastly, we must apply the Word of God in our lives.

Now you may ask isn't believing it enough? Isn't believing the true application?

When we apply the Word of God in our lives, then we are living out what we are believing God for. We know by faith that God will fulfill every promise He has made in our lives and so we live as though we already have the house, we live as though we have the job.

It's already done; we are just waiting on the manifestation. You must be convinced that faith works… and it does! Commit to live by faith. Decide that I am going to walk out this life according to the way God says I am supposed to live. I don't just want to be a Christian just getting by, but I want to flourish for my Lord Jesus. Then I will tell everybody that it was God that made the way for me and that as I walked by faith I was able to tap into God's best.

Walking by faith, is walking towards your Outpouring!

My Next Steps

1. _____

_____

_____

2. _____

_____

_____

3. _____

_____

_____

Notes

Chapter Five

Walk In Love

Outpouring

Experiencing The Fresh Power Of The Holy Spirit In Your Life!

"I Will Pour Out My Spirit..."
Acts 2:17

In order to experience the Outpouring, we must show love to one another. Hatred, jealousy, strife and any other negative emotions must not be exhibited toward one another.

Galatians 5:14
[14] For all the law is fulfilled in one word, even in this; Thou shalt love thy neighbor as thyself.

We should treat each other with kindness and compassion. We should treat each other the way we would want to be treated. It is the trick of the enemy for there to be dissension among us and hard feelings between us. These things distract us and keep us from experiencing the Outpouring.

So how do we walk in love? Forgive. Let go of past hurts. I know that's easier said than done but as you make the effort it will get easier and easier. Negative emotions toward someone else hinders your ability to focus on the things God wants to do in your life.

The enemy will bring the situation that caused the negative emotions to you over and over again. Unforgiveness holds you hostage to a past that you cannot change.

As you replay in your mind, the negative feelings get cemented into the foundation of your thinking. The time spent reviewing the wrong done or the hurt it caused is time not being used to focus on the things that build you up and push you further into your destiny.

Jesus loves us despite our mistakes and shortcomings. Jesus even showed love during the painful experience of the cross. While still hanging on the cross He forgave the criminal hanging beside Him.

He asked His Father to forgive those who were crucifying Him. Then he also designated someone to take care of His mother after He was gone. He showed love in the most painful of situations.

Jesus didn't want anything to clog the line between He and His Father. Neither should we allow anything to clog our opportunity to experience the Outpouring of the Holy Spirit.

Sometimes the world seems so cold and cruel. Everyone often seems to only be out for themselves without any consideration of others.

But that's not God's way. God wants us to love one another and be good to each other. This is when our Christian witness is the most evident. And this is when we can experience the Outpouring!

My Next Steps

1. _____

_____

_____

2. _____

_____

_____

3. _____

_____

_____

_____

Notes

Chapter Six

A Culture Of Anticipation

Outpouring

Experiencing The Fresh Power Of The Holy Spirit In Your Life!

"I Will Pour Out My Spirit..."
Acts 2:17

Get excited about who God is and what He is able to do! We should not drag around as Christians always down and out and weary. Instead we should be motivated, enthusiastic, and passionate. After all, we're children of the King!

Paul told Timothy in *2 Timothy 1:6-7 (KJV)*
[6] Wherefore I put thee in remembrance that thou stir up the gift of God, which is in thee by the putting on of my hands.
[7] For God hath not given us the spirit of fear; but of power, and of love, and of a sound mind.

"Stir up" can mean to keep blazing and to keep the flame of the fire burning. But it can also mean to rekindle and to re-stir the flame, indicating that the flame was about to go out.

Think about which meaning is applicable to you. God has deposited some things in you that you have allowed to lay dormant and if you want to experience the Outpouring you must get stirred up! You must fully utilize and move forward with boldness in the gifts God has given you.

In the text, Timothy received special gifts of the spirit that enabled him to serve the church. And God has given each of us gifts as well. Think about what you're good at. What do you really love to do? What has God directed you to do? Get busy!

There are also some areas all of us must stir up. Stir up the love in your life. Embrace people. Love people and do kind things for others. Stir up your faith. Have genuine, limitless faith. Believe God for big things. We do God an injustice when we play Him small. He is so much bigger than you could ever imagine. Stir up the power of God in your life. Let God use you. Totally surrender to His will and His way. Ask Him for His power and strength.

Stir up your mind. God has given us power, love, and a sound mind. Discipline your mind and your behavior. To have a sound mind is to have self control. A person with a sound mind masters their emotions and their behavior no matter what they may face. Does your behavior show you have a sound mind?

Paul told Timothy don't be ashamed to testify.

Sometimes we don't testify or tell others about God's goodness because we don't want to be viewed as a fanatic.

Or sometimes we don't want people to know about our past. But if you are ashamed to own Jesus before men He won't own you before the Father.

We must be willing to talk about how wonderful God is. Be passionate about the Lord and your walk with Him. Create a culture of anticipation in your life.

I wonder what God will do next? I wonder how God will work this out? I know He's going to do it! God has done so much already, and I know He is going to do even more*!*

Anticipate the Outpouring. Live open to the move and the blessing of the Holy Spirit. Live your life in anticipation of the Outpouring every day!

My Next Steps

1. _____

_____

_____

2. _____

_____

_____

3. _____

_____

_____

_____

Notes

Chapter Seven

Where Did It All Begin?

Outpouring

Experiencing The Fresh Power Of The Holy Spirit In Your Life!

"I Will Pour Out My Spirit..."
Acts 2:17

The prophet Joel said it first.

Joel 2: 28-29 (KJV)
[28] And it shall come to pass afterward, that I will pour out my spirit upon all flesh; and your sons and your daughters shall prophesy, your old men shall dream dreams, your young men shall see visions:
[29] And also upon the servants and upon the hand-maids in those days will I pour out my spirit.

God sent Joel to get the people to turn from their sins, so He could restore the nation. When they turned from their sins they would experience the outpour of the Spirit of God. Peter reiterated Joel's statement in *Acts 2:17-18* when he said *"And it shall come to pass in the last days, saith God, I will pour out of my Spirit upon all flesh: and your sons and your daughters shall prophesy, and your young men shall see visions, and your old men shall dream dreams: And on my servants and on my handmaidens I will pour out in those days of my Spirit; and they shall prophesy"*.

Peter adds that this Outpouring will happen in the last days. Peter was fresh out of the Upper Room where the great Outpouring of the Holy Spirit had just occurred.

The 120 who were gathered there were speaking in tongues and acting in ways no one had ever seen before. People immediately thought that they were drunk. That's so typical. Even today when you make a step for God people often try to make it into something negative. Instead of taking the time to find out in an unbiased way what you have experienced, they will write it off as something inappropriate, or weird, or strange.

But Peter set the record straight, without fear, but with the passion that comes when you've had an encounter with the Holy Spirit. Peter boldly stood up in Acts 2:16 and said, "This is that which was spoken by the prophet Joel"!

I can only imagine Peter's excitement. He was really saying don't you see? This is what we've been waiting for? He's here! The Holy Spirit is here and WOW, it's great to experience His POWER!!!!!

The line was drawn from Joel to Peter. Then Peter drew the line to us! We are living in the last days!

The same prophesy Joel gave thousands of years ago applies to us today! If we will return to God, we too can experience the Outpouring. Forsake sin. In other words, live according to God's Word.

Believe on the Lord Jesus Christ. Accept Him as Lord! Repent. Pray. Walk in Faith. Walk in Love. I hear you saying I'm not perfect. You don't have to be, just ask God for forgiveness and do your best to live the life of a Christian. God will do the rest.

You don't want to miss this. Our loved ones who believed and have gone before us and the saints of the ages are in the great cloud of witnesses in glory and are screaming "DON'T MISS IT!" It's our turn now. It's here! It's here NOW! It's the OUTPOURING!

My Next Steps

1. _____

_____

_____

2. _____

_____

_____

3. _____

_____

_____

_____

Notes

Chapter Eight

Total Surrender

Outpouring

Experiencing The Fresh Power Of The Holy Spirit In Your Life!

"I Will Pour Out My Spirit..."
Acts 2:17

This text from the book of Acts allows us to enter into a moment that is very powerful. One hundred and twenty believers are gathered in the upper room. There they prayed and waited for the promise Jesus had spoken of while He was still with them. Jesus told them of the arrival of the Holy Spirit and with great anticipation they waited.

John 14:16-17 (KJV)
[16] And I will pray the Father, and he shall give you another Comforter, that he may abide with you for ever;
[17] Even the Spirit of truth; whom the world cannot receive, because it seeth him not, neither knoweth him: but ye know him; for he dwelleth with you, and shall be in you.

John 15:26 (KJV)
[26] But when the Comforter is come, whom I will send unto you from the Father, even the Spirit of truth, which proceedeth from the Father, he shall testify of me:.

They were met by the Holy Ghost. This was who Jesus had promised would come. He told them, I will send you the Holy Ghost and that's Who met them in the upper room.

The Bible says that the Holy Ghost rested on them and they spoke in other tongues or languages.

Acts 2:4 (KJV)
[4] And they were all filled with the Holy Ghost, and began to speak with other tongues, as the Spirit gave them utterance.

There were people in town from several different countries. When the 120 came down from the upper room they were speaking in various languages. Even though these were common everyday people they fluently spoke in other languages. People said they must be drunk! They must be! How could they possibly be speaking in other languages?

Acts 2:7-8 (KJV)
[7] And they were all amazed and marvelled, saying one to another, Behold, are not all these which speak Galilaeans?
[8] And how hear we every man in our own tongue, wherein we were born?

Acts 2:11 (KJV)
[11] Cretes and Arabians, we do hear them speak in our tongues the wonderful works of God.

Peter stepped out front and said these are not drunk like you think they are. Instead Peter directed them to the scripture spoken so long ago by the prophet Joel in Joel 2:23.

Acts 2:14-17 (KJV)
[14] ¶ But Peter, standing up with the eleven, lifted up his voice, and said unto them, Ye men of Judaea, and all ye that dwell at Jerusalem, be this known unto you, and hearken to my words:
[15] For these are not drunken, as ye suppose, seeing it is but the third hour of the day.
[16] But this is that which was spoken by the prophet Joel;
[17] And it shall come to pass in the last days, saith God, I will pour out of my Spirit upon all flesh: and your sons and your daughters shall prophesy, and your young men shall see visions, and your old men shall dream dreams:

This group experienced the Outpouring of the Holy Spirit because they were totally surrendered. They made a dangerous journey going to the upper room. It was really risking their lives.

If the chief priests and Pharisees found out they were doing anything to keep the teachings of Jesus alive they could be persecuted or even executed.

However because they surrendered totally to Jesus and did not surrender to fear they experienced the great filling of the Holy Spirit.

They could have been anywhere! If they were at home grieving for Jesus no one would have been upset. Even if in the face of danger they decided to give up in order to keep their families safe, people would have understood.

But when you truly have an encounter with Jesus you realize that nothing is more important than being close to Him! Paul urged us to totally surrender and sacrifice all and live for Jesus.

Romans 12:1 (KJV)
I beseech, you therefore brethren, by the mercies of God, that ye present your bodies a living sacrifice. Holy, acceptable unto God. Which is your reasonable service.

Now, just as the 120 did, we must totally surrender our lives to God.

There are so many times when we surrender in life, but yet we don't want to surrender to God. When you fly on an airplane, you leave it to the pilot, and sit down and say, take me to the destination I've purchased the ticket for and you trust him to do that.

When you go to the doctor, you surrender to what medicine or procedure they feel is best for you. Why not surrender to the one who has been here from the beginning of time. Jesus loves you and has a plan for your life.

Jeremiah 29:11-13 (KJV)
[11] For I know the thoughts that I think toward you, saith the LORD, thoughts of peace, and not of evil, to give you an expected end.
[12] Then shall ye call upon me, and ye shall go and pray unto me, and I will hearken unto you.
[13] And ye shall seek me, and find me, when ye shall search for me with all your heart.

Why not surrender? Jeremiah tells us what God says about you. He is not here to condemn you, but He is here to bless you. When you repent He is here to take you in His arms and say, I forgive you.

I'll change your life. Someone has made us think that God is constantly looking to see how hard He can make our lives and how many burdens He can put on us!

Instead He is a loving Father who says come home. I love you! In order to experience the Outpouring, you must totally surrender in every area of your life. It's important not to hold anything back. Give God total control and allow Him to lead, guide, and direct you.

Surrender your mind. When you surrender your mind to God, it means processing your thoughts through the lens of the gospel.

Our faith is not irrational. Jesus will withstand the inspection of any scientist or philosopher who tries to discredit him. Historical records and historical artifacts back up the story of the gospel. There is proof positive in the Bible that God is real and it is correlated with history even though sometimes they do not want us to know that.

But you must study and always be ready to give an answer and summary of your faith. This relationship with God is so much more than emotion!

Delve into God's Word and then you will have the foundation needed to live the life of the believer. Sometimes Christians are the least studied of all of the religions. We read one verse over here and one verse over there and another one in the middle.

Unfortunately, often we never study God's Word. Our minds are constantly bombarded with messages and most of them are not ones that build us up spiritually.

By the time our young people reach college age they have seen more than 200,000 television commercials. The average 21 year old has seen over 10,000 hours of violent content.

The enemy is attacking our mind trying to fill it with content that draws us away from God.

But the Bible says, let this mind be in you, which was also in Christ Jesus.

You see your mind is complex. It's more than a computer and much more powerful than a computer. A computer you use over and over again, but it does not get stronger. Instead eventually, it becomes obsolete. But your mind as you use it over and over again, it becomes stronger and stronger.

Things that are repeated and listened to over and over become reinforced in your mind. What you remember influences how you carry yourself.

Surrender your mind. Still functioning effectively in society. Able to carry out my daily tasks with precision and success. But also making sure I am constantly also filling my mind with the things of God.

Philippians 4:8 (KJV)
[8] Finally, brethren, whatsoever things are true, whatsoever things are honest, whatsoever things are just, whatsoever things are pure, whatsoever things are lovely, whatsoever things are of good report; if there be any virtue, and if there be any praise, think on these things.

My Next Steps

1.

2.

3.

Notes

_____

_____

_____

_____

_____

_____

_____

_____

_____

_____

_____

_____

_____

_____

_____

_____

_____

Conclusion

The *Outpouring* is here! You can live in it every-day!

There are definitely times when we worship to-gether when the presence of the Lord is so rich and so powerful that we don't have the words to de-scribe it. When we all get on one accord seeking God's face for more of His presence, the Holy Spirit moves in a mighty way and don't want to leave the building. When we surrender ourselves to the over-flow; when we allow ourselves to be overwhelmed by the Holy Spirit we never want to leave that place.

There are going to be more and more of these kind of services in the days ahead, and we love it when it happens. However, don't miss the personal Outpour-ing that you can walk in as well. This may happen at home, in your car, on your job, in the mall wherever! Because when you put the components in place for the Outpouring; it can happen anytime, anywhere. You must cooperate and participate in your own per-sonal spiritual growth. No one can grow for you but you.

You must be intentional in your walk with the Lord. Make your relationship with Him a priority.

Undergird your life with the foundation of prayer. Pray about everything. Your next move. Your relationships. Your daily tasks. Pray about all of it! Even those things that you may deem as not important enough to pray about. God wants to hear it all! So tell Him!

Walk by faith. Trust God for His direction and guidance. Believe God for the impossible. Believe God for the miraculous.

Walk in love. You are the most like Jesus when you show love! Forgive and let go of negative feelings you have for others. Learn to love past 'it', whatever the 'it' may be. Decide to live with a sense of anticipation. Expect God to move. Expect God to make a way. Expect God to deliver. Enjoy the exquisite love and peace that only comes from God. Remember how it all began in Joel 2 and how Peter reiterated it in Acts 2 on the Day of Pentecost. Believe in the Holy Spirit! He is here to bless you! He is here to overflow in your life. He is here to strengthen you. He is here to love you. He is here.

The *Outpouring*....IT'S HERE!

Plan of Salvation

How You Can Receive Jesus Christ
As your Lord And Savior

If you would like to welcome Jesus Christ into your life, you can do so at any time, anywhere.

Consider these important facts:
God loves you and seeks a personal relationshp with you! Behold, I stand at the door and knock. If anyone hers My voice and opens the door, I will come in to him and dine with him, and he with Me. Revelation 3:20

The problem is: Everyone has been born into this world spiritually dead because of sin.
For the wages of sin is death, but the gift of God is etrnal life in Christ Jesus our Lord.
Romans 6:23

Jesus will forgive us of all sin, assuring us of eternity in Heaven! If we confess our sins, He is faithful and just to forgive us our sins and to cleanse us from all unrighteousness.
1 John 1:19

To receive Jesus, pray this prayer:
Lord Jesus, I'm a sinner. Please come into my life and forgive me of all sin. I believe You died for my sins and rose from the dead. Now, fill me with Your Holy Spirit and guide me from this day forward. Thank you, Lord, for saving me! **Amen**

Sonjia B. Dickerson

is a motivational speaker, author, gospel recording artist and Executive Pastor of the Dayspring Family Church located at 618 N. Belt Line Road in Irving, Texas, where her husband Bishop Kevin Dickerson is Senior Pastor. She has a Bachelors Degree in Accounting from Loyola University in Chicago, Illinois; Masters Degree in Biblical Studies as well as Doctor of Ministry from Vision International University. She is currently working on her Masters of Christian Leadership at Criswell College.

Dickerson also serves on various community boards and host and coordinates yearly women's conferences in and outside of the state of Texas. During her seven-year tenure at the Tarrant Area Food Bank, she served as the Kids Café Director and established more than 20 after school feeding sites for at risk children which served more than 1600 children a hot evening meal on a daily basis.

Sonjia B. Dickerson Ministries and Dayspring Family Church are partners with the North Texas Food Bank and provide food for residents in Irving and surrounding areas year around.

At Thanksgiving alone, they provide food boxes (that feed a family of 7) to over 2000 families. During the summer months Sonjia targets children at risk for hunger and leads a team that serves lunch to over 300 children in inner city apartment complexes.

She is also the Founder and Executive Director of C.L.A.S.S. Inc. (Cultivating Leaders Achieving Scholastic Success). The program provides students with leadership development training and awards a monetary scholarship to each graduate. To date, over 168 scholarships have been given to students through C.L.A.S.S., Inc.

Pastor Sonjia is the 2015 and 2017 Singing Pastor of the Year for KHVN Radio in Dallas, Texas and has five music projects available: Faith For The Journey,

In His Presence, Continuously Praise, and Word of God Speak, and her recent project The Best of Sonjia B. Dickerson-Music That Inspires.

She also has seven book releases, "Faith Through The Changes of Life", "Magnificent Marriage", "Prayers For A Magnificent Marriage, Speak The Promise and Not The Problem", "Moving Forward", "It's Your Time", The Mordecai Effect", "I SEE VICTORY: Overcoming The Obstacles To Your Destiny", including her most recent titled Outpouring.

She is a woman of foresight and capability, accompanied by a great love for the people of God.

She maintains a busy preaching schedule and ministers with enthusiasm and captures the heart and mind of the hearer. She speaks a sound word with a lively style that allows for the move of the Holy Spirit.

Pastor Sonjia's ability to usher in the presence of God to a waiting audience is nothing less than the anointing of the Lord.

Pastor Sonjia B. Dickerson is the mother of three, Kevin II, Cherese, and Faith, and the spiritual mother to the members of the Dayspring Family Church.

She is married to Bishop Kevin Keith Dickerson, her sweetheart.

For more information about Sonjia B. Dickerson Ministries visit www.sonjiadickerson.com.

Sonjia B. Dickerson
Ministries

PRODUCTS

MUSIC

The Best of Sonjia B. Dickerson-Music That Inspires
Word Of God Speak
Faith For The Journey
In His Presence
Continuously Praise

BOOKS

OUTPOURING
OUTPOURING DEVOTIONAL
I See Victory Devotional
The Mordecai Effect
It's Your Time
Moving Forward
Speak The Promise And Not The Problem
Magnificent Marriage
Prayers For A Magnificent Marriage
Faith Through The Changes Of Life

PREACHING MESSAGES

PRAYERS ON CD

Pastor Sonjia Dickerson

has been ministering for over 28 years and is well studied with various degrees in main stream and faith based arenas.

HER CALLING:
- Anointed Preacher
- Anointed Singer
- Recording Artist
- Founder-Women In God's Service
- Founder-Pastor's Wives Conference
- Founder-Outpouring Women's Conference
- Author
- Teacher
- Ministry Consultant

AVAILABLE FOR:
- Worship Services
- Women's Conferences
- Leadership Seminars
- Marriage Seminars
- Music Ministry
- Excellence In Ministry Teaching

STAY CONNECTED:
- Twitter: @pastorsonjia
- Like us on Facebook
- www.facebook.com/pastorsonjia
- Instagram: sonjiadickerson
- Pinterest: sonjiadickerson

FOR BOOKINGS:

web: sonjiadickerson.com
email: info@sonjiadickerson.com
email: outpouringwc@gmail.com
contact Outpouring Office
P. 972-313-9031
Sonjia B. Dickerson Ministries
P.O. Box 153866
Irving, Texas 75015

Join Sonjia B. Dickerson
LIVE SUNRISE
MIRACLE PRAYER
Ministry & Motivation each
Friday @ 6AM CST
STREAMING LIVE
facebook.com / pastor sonjia dickerson